Praying the Promises of God for Daily Blessings and Breakthrough

DANIEL C. OKPARA

Published By:

Better Life Media.

BETTER LIFE WORLD OUTREACH CENTER.

Website: www.BetterLifeWorld.org

Email: info@betterlifeworld.org

This title and others are available for quantity discounts for sale promotions, gifts and evangelism. Visit our website or email us to get started.

Any scripture quotation in this book is taken from the King James Version or New International Version, except where stated. Used by permission.

Contents

"Forever, O LORD, thy word is settled in heaven." - Psalm 119:89

FREE BONUS ...

Download These 4 Powerful Books Today for

FREE... And Take Your Relationship With

God to a New Level.

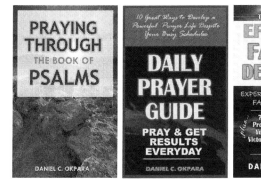 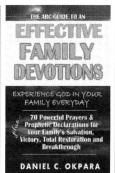 

www.betterlifeworld.org/grow

Thus Says the LORD,

"I will be your God through all your lifetime, yes, even when your hair is white with age. I made you and I will care for you. I will carry you along and be your Savior." - Isaiah 46:4 (TLB)

And we say...

"I believe Lord. Let it be unto me according to Thy Word"

Amen.

Introduction: "It Is Written!" The Power of Declaring Scriptures

Matthew 4:1-11 - *Then was Jesus led up of the Spirit into the wilderness to be tempted of the devil.*

And when he had fasted forty days and forty nights, he was afterward an hungred.

And when the tempter came to him, he said, If thou be the Son of God, command that these stones be made bread.

But he answered and said, It is written, Man shall not live by bread alone, but by every word that proceedeth out of the mouth of God.

Then the devil taketh him up into the holy city, and setteth him on a pinnacle of the temple,

And saith unto him, If thou be the Son of God, cast thyself down: for it is written, He shall give his angels charge concerning thee: and in their hands they shall bear thee up, lest at any time thou dash thy foot against a stone.

Jesus said unto him, It is written again, Thou shalt not tempt the Lord thy God.

Again, the devil taketh him up into an exceeding high

mountain, and sheweth him all the kingdoms of the world, and the glory of them;

And saith unto him, All these things will I give thee, if thou wilt fall down and worship me.

Then saith Jesus unto him, Get thee hence, Satan: for it is written, Thou shalt worship the Lord thy God, and him only shalt thou serve.

Then the devil leaveth him, and, behold, angels came and ministered unto him.

In this scripture, Jesus came face to face with satan, the arch enemy of man. And just as satan did in the gardedn of Eden, he started his subtle art of negotiations. He came up with ideas, suggestions and recommendations.

First, he said to Christ, "Hey, you must be very hungry. You have power to turn these stones into bread, so just do it."

Jesus recognized that this was a game. It was not a genuine interest in his hunger, but same old trick he used on the first Adam. So He replied,

"It is written…"

Over and out. One –zero (1-0)

Satan must have been very shocked. He was used to getting his way all the time with man. He had deceived Adam with same old strategy thousands of years earlier before Christ.

But not this time.

Next, he came up with another more subtle idea and included scripture too in his message.

"Jump down from this mountain. God will not allow you to dash your foot against a stone," he said.

Jesus smiled; and then replied…

"It is written…"

Wow!

Two-zero (2-0).

"Oh well, I get it," satan said, as he became more aggressive. "But since you came to save the world, let's make it easier and quicker. Bow down to me and I will just hand over to you the world immediately."

Jesus said again, "IT IS WRITTEN..."

Three-zero (3-0)

Satan couldn't take any more of it. He was defeated. He was knocked down and will remain defeated.

Three times the devil attacked Christ. Three times Christ declared the Word of God.

This story in the Bible is God showing us a pattern for handling the devil with all his lies and attacks.

> *"When the devil attacks you, declare the WORD of God and keep declaring it."*

It sounds like you've heard that before, right? Well, I guess. The fact is that the simplicity of God's truths does not deflate their power to bring about great changes.

The promises of God in the Bible have the power to defeat any negative situation that life throws at you. The promises have the power to overcome any attack that comes your way – be it in your mind, in your body, in your home, in your office – anywhere.

> *"For all the promises of God in him are*
> *yea, and in him Amen, unto the glory*
> *of God by us." - 2 Corinthians 1:20*

There are many, many promises of God in Scripture. In each promise, God pledges that something will (or will not) be done or given or come to pass. These are not dismissive, casual promises such as we often make; these promises of God are rock-solid, unequivocal commitments made by God Himself. Because God is faithful, the recipients of the divine promises can have full assurance that what God has pledged will indeed be realized

This small book is intended to share God's promises with you on various aspects of life. As your read these Bible verses about the promises of God, claim them over your life!

Freedom from addictions, deliverance from sin and evil, financial provision, hope for lost and hurting family and friends, overcoming depression, recovering a marriage, good health, healing, being free from fear and anxiety, strength, and many more are the blessings and gifts that God promises to provide for those who believe in Him.

Memorize the Scriptures that promise to overcome what you are facing today. Pray over them and speak them out loud and you will begin to see God move in your life for His glory and for your good!

Prayer 1: Psalm 91 – Divine Protection

₁"I live within the shadow of the Almighty, sheltered by the God who is above all gods.

₂ This I declare, that he alone is my refuge, my place of safety; he is my God, and I am trusting him completely.

₃ He rescues me from every trap of those chasing my life and destiny and protects me from deadly diseases.

₄He shields and shelters me with his wings! His truthful promises are my shield.

₅Henceforth, I will never be afraid for the terrors of the night, nor fear the dangers of the day; 6 nor dread the plagues of darkness, nor disasters in the noon day.

₇Though a thousand fall at my side, though ten thousand are dying around me, the evil one will not touch me. Premature death will not come close to my household

₈I will see how the wicked are punished, but I will not share in it.

₉For Jehovah is my refuge! I choose Him above all gods

to shelter me.

10 Evil will not come near my dwelling place. 11 For the angels are under instruction to protect me wherever I go. 12 They will protect me with their hands. I will not stumble or dash my foot against a stone.

13 When I meet a lion or step on poisonous snakes, yes, even trample them beneath my feet, no harm will befall me!

14 For the Lord says, "Because he loves me, He will rescue me; He will make me great because I put my trust in His name.

15 When I call on Him, He will answer; He will be with me in trouble and rescue me and honor me.

16 He will satisfy me with a full, healthy and long life and at the end, I will receive His salvation."

In Jesus name.

Amen

Lesson 1: Why Trust God And His Promises?

"So shall my word be that goeth forth out of my mouth: it shall not return unto me void, but it shall accomplish that which I please, and it shall prosper in the thing whereto I sent it." **- Isaiah 55:11**

God is known by His Word. He is everything the Word says He is, and He will do everything His Word says He will do.

If you want to find out who God is, go to the Word and find out. Sometimes people say, "I'm not sure if God will do this. I hope He will."

You don't have to be like that. If you want to find out

what God will do, go to the Word.

Why should one trust God and His promises?

1. His Words Have Been Purified

"The words of the Lord are pure words: as silver tried in a furnace of earth, purified seven times." - Psalm 12:6

Before God says anything, it must have gone through the crucible of refinement. His Words and promises can be trusted because they have been tried severally.

2. The Unchanging Nature of God and His Promises

Man can change at will, circumstances may force him to change and break his word or promise. But not so with God. *"God is not a man, that he should lie, nor a son of man, that he should change his mind. Does he speak and then not act? Does he promise and not fulfill?"* (Numbers 23:19).

Even though Balak had hired Balaam to place a curse on the Israelites in exchange for a reward, and though Balaam was willing to do so, he could not. Because he knew that God was committed to delivering the Israelites as He had promised. He told his paymaster point that God was committed to deliver and save Israel no matter what anybody does.

God's promises are sure. We can take them to the bank because He is committed to act and fulfill His Word.

3. God is One With His Words and Promises

"In the beginning was the Word, and the Word was with God, and the Word was God" (John 1:1).

You cannot separate God from His word.

4. His Word Cannot be Broken or Altered

"If he called them gods, unto whom the word of God came, and the scripture cannot be broken." - **John 10:35**

"My covenant will I not break, nor alter the thing that is gone out of my lips." - **Psalm 89:34**

5. God Cannot Lie

"That by two immutable things, in which it was impossible for God to lie, we might have a strong consolation, who have fled for refuge to lay hold upon the hope set before us." - ***Hebrews 6:18***

"And also the Strength of Israel will not lie nor repent: for he is not a man, that he should repent."
- 1 Samuel 15:29

*"Once have I sworn by my holiness that I will not lie unto David." - **Psalm 89:35***

6. God is on Oath to Perform His Word

For when God made promise to Abraham, because he could swear by no greater, he sware by himself,

Saying, Surely blessing I will bless thee, and multiplying I will multiply thee.

And so, after he had patiently endured, he obtained the promise.

For men verily swear by the greater: and an oath for confirmation is to them an end of all strife.

Wherein God, willing more abundantly to shew unto the heirs of promise the immutability of his counsel, confirmed it by an oath:

That by two immutable things, in which it was impossible for God to lie, we might have a strong consolation, who have fled for refuge to lay hold upon the hope set before us. - Hebrews 6:13-18

Prayer 2: Psalm 23 – Divine Guidance & Provision

"Heavenly Father, I thank You because You are my Shepherd,

And because You are my Shepherd, I have everything I need!

I am convinced that You are leading me always and will show me the right way, every day. So I know I am safe under Your protective care.

LORD, You know where true rest and blessings are found, and You will lead me there day by day.

Give me new strength every day and help me do what honors You the most. Enable me to live righteous for Your purpose and cause me to continue to walk in Your ways, as You draw me close to You.

Even when I walk through dark valleys and uncertain paths, I will not let fear control me. For I know that as the Good Shepherd, O LORD, You are always there, guarding and guiding me. Your Holy Spirit will lead me to Your Words where I will find rest and comfort for my soul at such times.

I may have many enemies who surround me, but LORD, You will always cause me to excel and succeed no matter what they do. Through Your blessings in my life and my share of love and joy of salvation, my life will bring others to Your saving grace."

Let Your Goodness and unfailing mercies and kindness continue to follow me as I serve You on this earth and will finally be with You in heaven, in Jesus name I pray.

Lesson 2: Conditions for Praying the Promises of God

"Whereby are given unto us exceeding great and precious promises: that by these ye might be partakers of the divine nature, having escaped the corruption that is in the world through lust"

- 2 Peter 1:4

One reason God has given us His promises is so we can escape the corruption of this world and be a partaker of His divine nature. However, if we're going to pray and manifest the promises of God efficiently, then we need to know a few things. For example, God has promised that you'll live long and fulfill your days. But if you intentionally jump in front of a train, you're going to get killed. So there are things we need to generally know and do to pray and manifest God's promises effectively.

1. Know His Promises

"And ye shall know the truth, and the truth shall make you free." **- John 8:32.**

It's the truth you know that will set you free.

And what is the truth?

The WORD.

John 17:17 says,

"Sanctify them through thy truth: thy word is truth."

If you are ignorant of the word, there is no way you will be able to apply them in your prayer and manifest them in your life. So the first basic requirement for praying and manifesting the promises of God is to read and know the promises. Then meditate on them and let them sink deep in you.

2. Believe the Promises

"But without faith it is impossible to
please Him. For he that cometh to
God must believe that He is, and that
He is a rewarder of those who
diligently seek Him."- *Hebrews 11:6*

Can I be honest with you?

It's very easy for us to shout, 'believe the promises.'

But from my experience, it needs work on ourselves to really believe. There have been times when I read a scripture and I'm like, "For real?"

The one that gets some fire in me mostly is Matthew 7: 9-11 which says,

> *Or what man is there of you, whom if*
> *his son ask bread, will he give him a*
> *stone?*

Or if he ask a fish, will he give him a serpent?

If ye then, being evil, know how to give good gifts unto your children, how much more shall your Father which is in heaven give good things to them that ask him?

Look at that scripture. Of a truth, if my son, Isaac, asks me for bread, I won't give him a stone. And if he asks me for a fish, I won't give him a snake. I also think most parents won't either. So when I read this place, I ask myself, *"Lord, please don't be offended. But what exactly are you saying here, because I have asked You for so many things that I didn't get?"*

I'm sure most of us have asked something similar. But if you allow the Holy Spirit to talk to you about it, you'll begin to get that what God is saying there is really beyond asking and getting things.

First, you'll realize that *"His divine power hath given unto us all things that pertain unto life and godliness, through the knowledge of Him that hath called us to glory and virtue"* (1 Peter 1:3). This means that whatever I'm going to ask for has already been provided. I only need to know what to do to appropriate it. So my prayer will now be *"LORD, show my by Your Spirit what I need to do to manifest this promise I'm believing you for"*

You'll now realize that God isn't intimidated when we ask Him for anything – not even money. Yes, I used to think that we can't and shouldn't ask God for money. But you see, we can. More importantly however, we need to realize that He has provided all the money we'll ever need here on earth. Now, what we need is to prayerfully discern what we need to do to appropriate as much as we need.

Secondly, you'll see that there are stages in the asking

process. As an under 2-year old, I'll surely get Isaac all that he wants. But as he grows, he'll need to start learning how to do things for Himself. A time comes, he'll need to step out there, face his challenges, overcome them and be the man. Now that doesn't mean that I'm no longer his Dad. I'm surely there, providing for him, guiding him, empowering him. But letting him do the stuff by himself.

If you're going to pray and manifest the promises of God for yourself, you'll need to, and must, believe them. Where you're overwhelmed, you can pray like I do, *"LORD, please what are You really saying here? Teach me."* The Holy Spirit will teach you and your life will change with the revelation you'll get.

The point is that we must believe in the promises of God regarding our needs that we are praying about. And if you are finding it hard to really believe the promises, then just talk to God about the difficulty you're having.

Most times also, I just tell the LORD my doubts. I say, *"Lord, I'm not happy. I think I have some doubts in me about this, because I have had really bad experiences. Please help me to believe You on this because Your Words are Yea and Amen. Thank You for helping me to believe You enough."*

Then I speak to myself over and over and over. I say, *"Dan, you'll need to believe this. This is true. You'll surely see the reality of it."*

I don't know if theologians will frown at that but, hey, God is our father. He knows our weaknesses and struggles. When we are struggling to believe, we can tell Him about it and the Holy Spirit will move in our hearts in a powerful way

3. Confess Your Sins to God and Forsake Them

"But your iniquities have separated between you and your God, and your sins have hid his face from you, that he will not hear" - Isaiah 59:2

Sin can, and does, stand in the way between us and our

prayers. Ask the Holy Spirit to search you and bring to your knowledge any sin that you need to confess and do something about.

4. Practice Forgiveness

"And when ye stand praying, forgive, if ye have ought against any: that your Father also which is in heaven may forgive you your trespasses" - Mark 11:23-25.

Unforgiveness works more against us than those we refuse to forgive. Again, we can be real with God on this. If the pain is much we can say,

> *"LORD, you see that? You see this person has really offended me so much. I'm not happy right now and I feel like revenging this. But You've said I should forgive.*
>
> *Please Lord, will you help me to forgive him? I actually don't feel like forgiving but I am trusting You to take away this*

> *pain and bitterness in my heart and to invest your love in me, so I can forgive and forget this and move on. For I know You have good plans for me.*
>
> *Thank You LORD"*

Don't wait until you feel like forgiving before you forgive offences and hurts against you. Pray to God and receive His grace to forgive in advance and move on.

Without forgiveness, we cannot pray and manifest the promises of God in our lives.

5. Learn to Obey the Leading of the Holy Spirit

In my book, How God Speaks to You, I said, "the secret of the miraculous is in following the leading of the Holy Spirit."

For example, God has promised to protect us, but many Christians still die in accidents. Why?

Simple.

Many times we fail to manifest the promises of God for our lives because we don't learn to follow the leading of the Holy Spirit.

> *But the Comforter, which is the Holy Ghost, whom the Father will send in my name, he shall teach you all things, and bring all things to your remembrance, whatsoever I have said unto you.* – **John 14:26**

We all need to learn How to Discern and Hear the Voice Of God in our daily lives, for in following the voice of God will we effectively pray and manifest the promises of God.

6. Obedient Walk in the Word of God

> *"For it is not those who hear the law who are righteous in God's sight, but it is those who obey the law who will*

*be declared righteous" **(Rom 2:13)***

---

*"He that saith, I know him, and keepeth not his commandments, is a liar, and the truth is not in him. - **1 John 2:4***

We must learn to accept God's Word as the final authority in our lives to really get to know God through prayer. *God will not listen to a person who rebels and persistently disobeys His Word.* If you come to God in a humble, repentant spirit and are determined to obey Him to the best of your knowledge and ability, He will hear your prayers.

7. You Must Go to God in Faith

"And without faith it is impossible to please God because anyone who come to him must believe that he exist and that he rewards those who earnestly seek him" (Hebrews 11:6)

"This is the confidence we have in approaching God: that if we ask anything according to his will, he hears us. 15. And if we know that he hears us—whatever we ask—we know that we have what we asked of him" (1 John 5:14, 15)

It is not enough to pray, you must believe to receive your request. Trust God to make it good- his promises. Prayer is useless without faith, because your faith must be tied to the promise.

8. Be Persistent

Now Jesus was telling the disciples a parable to make the point that at all times they ought to pray and not give up and lose heart, ₂ saying, "In a certain city there was a judge who did not fear God and had no respect for man.

₃ There was a [desperate] widow in that city and she kept coming to him and saying, 'Give me justice and legal protection from my adversary.'

₄For a time he would not; but later he said to himself, 'Even though I do not fear God nor respect man, ₅ yet because this widow continues to bother me, I will give her justice and legal protection; otherwise by continually coming she [will be an intolerable annoyance and she] will wear me out.'"

₆ Then the Lord said, "Listen to what the unjust judge says!

₇And will not [our just] God defend andavenge His elect [His chosen ones] who cry out to Him day and night? Will He delay [in providing justice] on their behalf?

₈ I tell you that He will defend and avenge them quickly. However, when the Son of Man comes, will He find [this kind of persistent] faith on the earth?" – Luke 18: 1-8

Prayer 3: Comfort Psalms: Prayer of Comfort

Heavenly Father,

There are many prayers I have prayed, many times I have cried to Thee. Lord, I know that You heard me and have reached out to me.

You alone know all my fears and tossings. They are right before thy eyes.

You are my refuge and strength, a very present help in trouble. You will help me out of whatever trouble I face right now and in the future. By Your Spirit, You will show me what to do, where to go and how to respond to these times

So I cast all my burden on Thee, for according to Thy Word, You will not allow your own to be moved.

For Your anger is but for a moment, Your favor is for life.

My tears and weeping is only for a moment, it may endure for a night, but I am certain that joy comes in the morning."

Lord, please heal my heart where it is broken right now, and bind up my wounds with Your love and power.

Deliver me from all that trouble me at the moment. And let your peace, hope, assurance and comfort fill my heart this day and every day, in Jesus name I pray.

Based on the Following Psalms of Comfort.

Psalms 22:24 - For he has not despised or abhorred the affliction of the afflicted, and he has not hidden his face from him, but has heard, when he cried to him.

Psalms 56:8 - You have kept count of my tossings; put my tears in your bottle. Are they not in your book?

Psalms 116:1-2 - I love the LORD, because he has heard my voice and my pleas for mercy. Because he inclined his ear to me, therefore I will call on him as long as I live.

Psalms 46:1 - God is our refuge and strength, a very present help in trouble.

Psalms 55:22 - Cast your burden on the LORD, and he will sustain you; he will never permit the righteous to be moved.

Psalm 30:5: "For His anger is but for a moment, His favor is for life; weeping may endure for a night, but joy comes in the morning."

Psalm 147:3 - "He heals the brokenhearted and binds up their wounds."

Psalm 34:19 (NIV) - The righteous person may have many troubles, but the LORD delivers him from them all.

Lesson 3: How to Pray the Promises of God

There are promises that cover whatever area of challenge you may currently be facing. Do you need healing? Wisdom? The ability to pay the bills? Whatever it is, you can pray one of God's promises that relates to your issue, and hold onto it.

1. Find the Promises that Relate to Your Situation.

Many years ago, I read a story that challenged me a lot. It was about the wife of a prominent man of God who fell sick and was told by the experts that she had only few days to live – based on their diagnosis and analysis. Her husband, a powerful preacher, prayed and prayed and invited other men of God to pray, yet nothing happened. Her case continued to worsen.

With just few days to the experts' date remaining, this woman mustered some strength, settled down and located forty scriptures on God's health and healing plan. As she continued to read, meditate on and minister to herself with those scriptures, the sickness (whatever they called it) eventually disappeared. She was healed and returned to her business.

Like I said, the word of God is not just a literature. It carries life. If you are having any attack of illness in your body, rather than worry and fear, <u>locate God's Words about your health</u> and stay with them for some time.

The same thing applies to any area that you may be having a challenge. Make a compilation of verses that speak on those areas, and begin to do battle with those scriptures.

2. Meditate on the promises

"This Book of the Law shall not depart from your mouth, but you shall read [and meditate on] it day and night, so that you may be careful to do [everything] in accordance with all that is written in it; for then you will make your way prosperous, and then you will be successful" - Joshua 1:8 (AMP)

To mediate means to think deeply and carefully about something for a period of time. Focus your mind on the promise that you are trusting God for, and think about the WORD for a while. Let the truths permeate your soul. Then you'll see how great a God you serve!

3. Personalize the Promises in Prayers

Take the promises you read and make them yours. For example, if you are praying for healing and you read somewhere like Isaiah 53:5 which says,

"But he was wounded for our transgressions, he was bruised for our iniquities: the chastisement of our peace was upon him; and with his stripes we are healed."

Personalizing this scripture, you'll begin to pray, say, *"LORD Jesus, You were wounded for my transgressions, bruised for my iniquities, chastised that I may have peace, and by your stripes, I am healed. So I claim my healing this day, in Jesus name"*

Same applies for any other area you are looking forward for a divine intervention. Locate the scriptures that promise you deliverance on them, meditate on the scriptures, personalize them and begin to do battle with them.

4. Declare the Promises Daily In Faith

But what saith it? The word is nigh thee, even in thy mouth, and in thy heart: that is, the word of faith, which we preach;

That if thou shalt confess with thy mouth the Lord Jesus, and shalt believe in thine heart that God hath raised him from the dead, thou shalt be saved.

For with the heart man believeth unto righteousness; and with the mouth confession is made unto salvation. - **Romans 10:8-10**

Verse 9 says that if you "confess with thy mouth the Lord Jesus, and shalt believe in thine heart that God hath raised him from the dead, thou shalt be saved." Jesus Christ is the Word of God. So that's simply saying, *"If you confess the word of God and believe that the Word is greater than your grave situations, you'll be saved"*

2 Corinthians 4:13 says, "It is written: 'I believed; therefore, I have spoken.' Since we have that same spirit

of faith, we also believe and therefore speak."

In other words, through faith confession one can lay claim and receive the promise of God. Talk or confess the Word till it becomes a reality for you.

Our words are like seeds. What we speak determines what we eventually see as harvest. This was the reason Abram's name was changed to Abraham so it can register in his spirit that he was a father of many nations even when he had no son.

You can't afford to be careless with your tongue and expect to live in the blessings of God. "For by your words you will be acquitted, and by your words you will be condemned" (Matthew 12:37).

5. Pray in the Holy Ghost

*In the same way, the Spirit helps us in
our weakness. We do not know what
we ought to pray for, but the Spirit
himself intercedes for us through
wordless groans.*

*And he who searches our hearts knows
the mind of the Spirit, because the
Spirit intercedes for God's people in
accordance with the will of God. (Rom
8:26-27)*

The Spirit is given to help us in our weakness. When we pray in the Holy Ghost, the Spirit is helping us to pray. And the spirit of God cannot pray amiss, but in the very will of God.

Sometimes one is not able to express himself adequately by words in prayer, considering the enormity of the need to be met. That is the time to turn it over to the Lord by praying in the Spirit, otherwise the devil can take unnecessary advantage of you.

Pray in other tongues and put him far away from you. Praying in tongues will align your prayer with the will of God and guarantee the answer to your prayer.

6. Use the Power of Praise and Worship

Let the people praise thee, O God; let all the people praise thee. O let the nations be glad and sing for joy: for thou shalt judge the people righteously, and govern the nations upon earth. Selah.

Let the people praise thee, O God; let all the people praise thee. Then shall the earth yield her increase; and God, even our own God, shall bless us. God shall bless us; and all the ends of the earth shall fear him. **- Psalm 67:3-7**

Praise is a powerful means of claiming God's promises.

When praise goes up, blessings come down.

One way you can pray the promises of God is to praise God for the promises you are praying for, declaring and believing.

You'll find in scripture that in very difficult times of war, the people of God were instructed to turn to praise with all manner of instruments. And as they did, God's heavenly army appears on the scene and gives them victory.

Learn to turn to praise from time to time and you'll have the victory that you seek

7. Exercise Patience

*"You need to persevere so that when
you have done the will of God, you will
receive what he has promised. For in
just a little while, he who is coming will
come and will not delay. But my
righteous one will live by faith. And I*

take no pleasure in the one who shrinks back" - Hebrews 10:36-39.

Why do we need to have patience? Because some of these promises might take some time before they manifest. There can be various reasons why, either known or unknown. Regardless of what your situation looks like today, remember that He is faithful, and He has promised to never leave or forsake you.

Prayer 4: Prayers for Career, Job, Business and Financial Breakthrough.

A. Submission/Surrender

"Heavenly Father, I give You praise because You delight in the prosperity of Your people. I give You praise because YOU supply my needs according to Your riches in Christ Jesus. .

"How often do I think that prosperity, money and success is by my own efforts and volition alone. LORD, I come to YOU this day and confess my ignorance and pride. Forgive me for not giving YOU the ultimate place in my finances in the past. Forgive me and let Your mercy prevail over me this day, in Jesus name.

By the Blood of Jesus, I receive forgiveness of sins. I receive forgiveness from any form of greed and financial impropriety in the past. LORD Jesus let Your Blood speak for me spiritually from this moment onwards.

"Thank YOU LORD Jesus because in YOU I have forgiveness of sins. In YOU I have grace to appear before the Almighty God to obtain mercy and find grace in time of need.

In YOU Lord Jesus, I have assurance that I'll receive answers for my prayers for my career, finances, business and job.

All Glory is to Your Name alone LORD.

B. Grace to Obey God's Prosperity Command

"Almighty Father, as it is written in Your WORD, in Job 36:11, that if I obey and serve YOU, that I will spend my days in prosperity and my years in plenty. LORD, I come to YOU this day and ask for grace to obey YOUR Word on finances and in every aspect of life henceforth.

"HOLY SPIRIT, I come to YOU today, I ask You to make me willing and obedient to the WORD of God henceforth according to Isaiah 1:19 so that I may eat

the good things of the land.

Please uproot every seed of greed and disobedience from my life this day.

Make me a blessing in this world, that my life will be a light and support to those who are in need, for it is written that when I give, You will command men to give back to me.

Inspire me to give and to give joyfully without regrets from today forward.

"Holy Spirit, please motivate me and help me to honor the LORD with my resources and finances from this day, so that my barns will be full and overflowing with harvest, in Jesus name."

C. Rebuke the Devil Over Your Finances

"Heavenly Father, I stand in the authority in the name of Jesus Christ right now. I command every demon working against my business, my career and my

finances to collapse, be bound and cast into the abyss.

"It is written in Matthew 16:19 that whatsoever I bind here on earth is bound in heaven and whatsoever I loose here on earth is loosed in heaven.

I therefore bind every spirit of poverty, lack, frustration and loss. I cast them into the abyss from today, in Jesus name.

"O LORD, based on Your Word we have authority here on this earth and according to (Mark 11:23) we can speak to the mountain and it will have to obey us.

So devil, I speak to you in the name of Jesus Christ, I command you to take your hands off my finances right now and every day.

"I speak to the mountain of Lack and Want, I command you to be removed and cast into the sea from this day forward, in the Name of Jesus.

"I hereby declare all curses against my life null, void, and destroyed from today.

In the name of Jesus Christ, I am redeemed from the curse of poverty! I am free from oppression.

I now loose the abundance of God, and all that

rightfully belongs to me now to start locating me, in Jesus name.

Let the abundance of the sea, the land and the heavenly places come to my abode from now onwards, in Jesus name.

I thank You O LORD that You have a plan for me to overcome lack and have abundance.

I now cast all my cares and money worries over on You Lord. I WILL NOT WORRY anymore, neither will I FRET. I have peace and I'm enjoying Your divine supplies.

"It is written that angels are ministering spirits sent to minster unto the heirs of salvation. Therefore LORD, I ask that your angels of goodness, love and success begin to minister to my needs henceforth, in the name of Jesus Christ.

"Wherever my finances are, whoever is connected to my financial breakthroughs, O LORD, let your angels begin to reconnect them to me this day. As I step out for work, business or on my career, LORD Jesus, men and women will bring me favor, in Jesus' name.

D. Receive the Power to Create Wealth.

Heavenly Father, it is written that You give us power to create wealth. Therefore, I ask You to give me the power, wisdom and guidance to create wealth in my life.

"LORD, I ask for ideas, I ask YOU for inspiration and divine strategies to turn my career around and grow my business into a global brand. Show me secrets hidden from men and help me to unleash YOUR full potential in what I am doing at the moment.

"O LORD, make me an employer of labor, so that I will be a blessing to others and fulfill the covenant of Abraham which I inherit in Christ Jesus. Direct me to men, women and materials that YOU have assigned to bring me into my place of financial and business dominion before the world began, in Jesus name.

"Holy Spirit, You are my teacher. I ask You to teach me how to make profit in my business and career. Teach me to become a shining light in my business and career. Open my eyes to the right job opportunities and profitable business ventures, in Jesus name.

D. Command the Blessings.

Heavenly Father, I thank YOU for Your Word, in Psalm 1:3, which says that I am like a tree planted by the riverside. Whatever I do prospers.

I therefor pray Lord, let your blessing and prosperity fill my house from this day forward..

"It is written in 1 Corinthians 9: 8 that God is able to make all grace abound toward me; that I, always having all sufficiency in all things, may abound to every good work.

"Therefore, LORD, I decree that from this day, I have all sufficiency in all things and I lack nothing. I decree that the grace of God is causing me to abound in every good work.

"It is written in Psalm 112:3 that wealth and riches will be in my house, and his righteousness endures forever.

"So I decree that my house shall be filled with wealth and riches in Jesus name".

"The Lord is my Shepherd. He prepares a table before me in the presence of my enemies. He anoints my head

with oil. My cup runs over with blessings!

Money comes to me right now. God is opening the windows of heaven for me. He meets my every need according to His riches in glory by Jesus Christ.

He is causing men to give unto me good measure, pressed down, shaken together and running over.

God has given me the power to get wealth. I'm blessed in the field. I am blessed going in and going out. I have the favor of God. Favor, breakthrough, success, money and every good thing comes to me from this day, in Jesus name.

Prayers Based on the Following Scriptures and Others.

Luke 6:38 - Give, and it shall be given unto you; good measure, pressed down, and shaken together, and running over, shall men give into your bosom. For with the same measure that ye mete withal it shall be measured to you again.

Psalm 35:27 (KJV) - Let them shout for joy, and be glad, that favour my righteous cause: yea, let them say continually,

Let the LORD be magnified, which hath pleasure in the prosperity of his servant.

Deuteronomy 8:18 - *But thou shalt remember the LORD thy God: for [it is] he that giveth thee power to get wealth, that he may establish his covenant which he sware unto thy fathers, as [it is] this day.*

Philippians 4:19 - But my God shall supply all your need according to his riches in glory by Christ Jesus.

3 John 1:2 - Beloved, I wish above all things that thou mayest prosper and be in health, even as thy soul prospereth.

2 Corinthians 9:8 - And God [is] able to make all grace abound toward you; that ye, always having all sufficiency in all [things], may abound to every good work.

Psalms 1:1-3 - And he shall be like a tree planted by the rivers of water, that bringeth forth his fruit in his season; his leaf also shall not wither; and whatsoever he doeth shall prosper.

Lesson 4: Now, Pray the Promises of God for Your Life

Below are some examples of God's promises on various areas that you can read, meditate on, personalize, pray with and hold onto. Of course, the promises of God cover every aspect of life. The ones listed here are just to get you started. If there is a specific area you are looking for that is not listed here, try an internet search.

For example, if I am looking for **God's promises on repaying debt**, what I would do is go to Google and type that phrase. It will throw up a lot of results, both necessary and unnecessary ones. I would then take some minutes to visit some of the websites and copy out scriptures that I feel relate to my situation. Afterwards, I would close the websites, close the computer or phone, and then get to my quiet place, re-read these scriptures and start meditating on them. Any insight or revelation that comes to my heart, I would write them down, personalize the scriptures one after another and begin to pray them to God and to myself.

By the time you do this several days, gradually, your heart will begin to sense what you'll need to do to manifest the promises that you are praying and declaring. And you will experience the reality of God's power in His Words.

Find it (1): God's Promises for Healing

Memory Verse:

"Worship the LORD your God, and His blessing will be

on your food and water. I will take away sickness from

among you." - Exodus 23:25

Comment

When praying for healing, there are a few things you can

do in the process:

1. Call the elders in the church to pray with you
   (James 5:14-15)

2. Continue to anoint yourself daily until you are
   completely restored

3. Continue to administer the Holy Communion to yourself daily and declare your faith in body and blood of Christ for restoration (John 6:56). I have taught about the power of the communion severally.

Then you can use these scriptures to pray for yourself or your loved ones. You're going to speak to your spirit, soul and body and declare your perfect health in Christ Jesus.

Healing Scriptures for Reflection.

Deuteronomy 7:15 - The Lord will keep you free from every disease. He will not inflict on you the horrible diseases you knew in Egypt.

Exodus 15:26 - He said, "If you will diligently listen to the voice of the Lord your God, and do that which is right in his eyes, and give ear to his commandments and keep all his statutes, I will put none of the diseases on you that I put on the Egyptians, for I am the Lord, your healer."

~

1 Peter 2:24 - Who his own self bare our sins in his own body on the tree, that we, being dead to sins, should live unto righteousness: by whose stripes ye were healed.

Jeremiah 33:6 - Behold, I will bring it health and cure, and I will cure them, and will reveal unto them the abundance of peace and truth.

Isaiah 53:5 - But he [was] wounded for our transgressions, [he was] bruised for our iniquities: the chastisement of our peace [was] upon him; and with his stripes we are healed.

James 5:14-15 - Is any sick among you? Let him call for the elders of the church; and let them pray over him, anointing him with oil in the name of the Lord:

And the prayer of faith shall save the sick, and the Lord shall raise him up; and if he have committed sins, they shall be forgiven him.

Matthew 10:8 - Heal the sick, cleanse the lepers, raise the dead, cast out devils: freely ye have received, freely give.

Deuteronomy 7:15 - And the LORD will take away from thee all sickness, and will put none of the evil diseases of Egypt, which thou knowest, upon thee; but will lay them upon all them that hate thee.

3 John 1:2 - "Beloved, I wish above all things that thou mayest prosper and be in health, even as thy soul prospereth"

Psalm 103:2-4 - Bless the LORD, O my soul, and forget not all his benefits: Who forgiveth all thine iniquities; who healeth all thy diseases; Who redeemeth thy life from destruction; who crowneth thee with lovingkindness and tender mercies.

Find it (2): God's Promises for Provision

Memory Verse:

"The young lions suffer want and hunger; but those who seek the LORD lack no good thing." - **Psalms 34:10**

Comment

God knows our needs and the Bible tells us of how God wants us to come to him with every need and care and worry that we may have. We can certainly talk to God about our physical needs, as well as our emotional and spiritual needs. As we maintain focus seeking Him, the Holy Spirit will speak to us too. And He will meet us at the very point of our needs.

Scriptures on God's Provision

Luke 12:24 - *"Consider the ravens: they neither sow nor reap, they have neither storehouse nor barn, and yet God feeds them. Of how much more value are you than the birds!"*

Genesis 3:21 - And the LORD God made for Adam and for his wife garments of skins and clothed them.

Genesis 9:3 - Every moving thing that lives shall be food for you. And as I gave you the green plants, I give you everything.

Exodus 14:22 - And the people of Israel went into the midst of the sea on dry ground, the waters beinga wall to them on their right hand and on their left.

Job 38:41 - Who provides for the raven its prey, when its young ones cry to God for help, and wander about for lack of food?

Psalms 34:10 - The young lions suffer want and hunger; but those who seek the LORD lack no good thing.

Psalms 81:10 - I am the LORD your God, who brought you up out of the land of Egypt. Open your mouth wide, and I will fill it.

Psalms 84:11 - For the LORD God is a sun and shield; the LORD bestows favor and honor. No good thing does he withhold from those who walk uprightly.

Matthew 6:31-32 - Therefore do not be anxious, saying, 'What shall we eat?' or 'What shall we drink?' or 'What shall we wear?' For the Gentiles seek after all these things, and your heavenly Father knows that you need them all.

Treasure Chest

Psalm 23:1-6 - The LORD is my shepherd; I shall not want.

He maketh me to lie down in green pastures: he leadeth me beside the still waters.

He restoreth my soul: he leadeth me in the paths of righteousness for his name's sake.

Yea, though I walk through the valley of the shadow of death, I will fear no evil: for thou art with me; thy rod and thy staff they comfort me.

Thou preparest a table before me in the presence of mine enemies: thou anointest my head with oil; my cup runneth over.

Surely goodness and mercy shall follow me all the days of my life: and I will dwell in the house of the LORD for ever.

Philippians 4:19 - And my God will supply every need of yours according to his riches in glory in Christ Jesus.

Matthew 7:7,11 - Ask, and it will be given to you; seek, and you will find; knock, and it will be opened to you...If you then, who are evil, know how to give good gifts to your children, how much more will your Father who is in heaven give good things to those who ask him!

Matthew 21:22 - And whatever you ask in prayer, you will receive, if you have faith."

John 14:13-14 - Whatever you ask in my name, this I will do, that the Father may be glorified in the Son. If you ask meanything in my name, I will do it.

John 15:7 - If you abide in me, and my words abide in you, ask whatever you wish, and it will be done for you.

John 15:16 - You did not choose me, but I chose you and appointed you that you should go and bear fruit and that your fruit should abide, so that whatever you ask the Father in my name, he may give it to you.

John 16:23-24 - In that day you will ask nothing of me. Truly, truly, I say to you, whatever you ask of the Father in my name, he will give it to you. Until now you have asked nothing in my name. Ask, and you will receive, that your joy may be full.

Romans 8:32 He who did not spare his own Son but gave him up for us all, how will he not also with him graciously give us all things?

1 John 3:22 - and whatever we ask we receive from him, because we keep his commandments and do what pleases him.

Find it (3): God's Promises for Protection

Memory Verse:

"But the Lord is faithful, and He will strengthen you [setting you on a firm foundation] and will protect and guard you from the evil one." - 2 Thessalonians 3:3 (AMP)

Comment

The world is increasingly becoming a more dangerous place to live. However, Our God is the great Protector. He is Jehovah Nissi, which means the LORD who guards, delivers, covers, preserves, shelters and watches over us. Sometimes we need to call upon Him in our prayers for protection.

Prayer

Father LORD I thank Thee because You are faithful. Your Word is Yeah and Amen.

I pray this day according to Your Word that You strengthen me and set me up on a firm foundation. Remind me always of Your power of protection and deliverance.

Let the reality of Your Word be continually made manifest in my life and family.

Protect and guard me and my home from the evil one. May our going out and our coming in continue to be a blessing. May the discusses and hidden plots and agreements of the enemy against us continue to remain frustrated perpetually, in Jesus name.

More Protection Scriptures

Isaiah 43:7 - When thou passest through the waters, I will be with thee; and through the rivers, they shall not overflow thee: when thou walkest through the fire, thou shalt not be burned; neither shall the flame kindle upon thee.

Psalm 138:7 - Though I walk in the midst of trouble, you preserve my life; you stretch out your hand against the wrath of my enemies, and your right hand delivers me.

Isaiah 41:10 - Fear thou not; for I [am] with thee: be not dismayed; for I am thy God: I will strengthen thee; yea, I will help thee; yea, I will uphold thee with the right hand of my righteousness.

Psalms 91:1-16 - He that dwelleth in the secret place of the most High shall abide under the shadow of the Almighty. (Read all...)

2 Timothy 4:18 - And the Lord shall deliver me from every evil work, and will preserve me unto his heavenly kingdom: to whom be glory for ever and ever. Amen.

Proverbs 19:23 - The fear of the LORD tendeth to life: and he that hath it shall abide satisfied; he shall not be visited with evil.

2 Thessalonians 3:3 - But the Lord is faithful, who shall stablish you, and keep you from evil.

Isaiah 54:17 - No weapon that is formed against thee shall prosper; and every tongue that shall rise against thee in judgment thou shalt condemn. This is the heritage of the servants of the LORD, and their righteousness is of me, saith the LORD.

2 Samuel 22:3-4 - The God of my rock; in him will I trust: he is my shield, and the horn of my salvation, my high tower, and my refuge, my saviour; thou savest me from violence.

James 4:7 - Submit yourselves therefore to God. Resist the devil, and he will flee from you.

Psalms 46:1 - ...God is our refuge and strength, a very present help in trouble.

Get in Touch

We love testimonies. We love to hear what God is doing around the world as people draw close to Him in prayer. Please share your story with us.

Also, please consider giving this book a review on Amazon and checking out our other titles at: www.amazon.com/author/danielokpara .

I also invite you to checkout our website at www.BetterLifeWorld.org and consider joining our newsletter, which we send out once in a while with great tips, testimonies and revelations from God's Word for a victorious living.

Feel free to drop us your prayer request. We will join faith with you and God's power will be released in your life and the issue in question

Other Books By the Same Author

1. Prayer Retreat: 21 Days Devotional With 500 Powerful Prayers & Declarations to Destroy Stubborn Demonic Problems, Dislodge Every Spiritual Wickedness Against Your Life and Release Your Detained Blessings

2. HEALING PRAYERS & CONFESSIONS: Powerful Daily Meditations, Prayers and Declarations for Total Healing and Divine Health.

3. 200 Violent Prayers for Deliverance, Healing and Financial Breakthrough.

4. Hearing God's Voice in Painful Moments: 21 Days Bible Meditations and Prayers to Bring Comfort, Strength and Healing When Grieving for the Loss of Someone You Love.

5 . Healing Prayers: 30 Powerful Prophetic Prayers that Brings Healing and Empower You to Walk in Divine Health.

6. Healing WORDS: 55 Powerful Daily Confessions & Declarations to Activate Your Healing & Walk in Divine Health: Strong Decrees That Invoke Healing for You & Your Loved Ones

7. <u>Prayers That Break Curses and Spells and Release Favors and Breakthroughs</u>.

8. <u>7 Days Fasting With 120 Powerful Night Prayers for Personal Deliverance and Breakthrough.</u>

9. <u>100 Powerful Prayers for Your Teenagers:</u> Powerful Promises and Prayers to Let God Take Control of Your Teenagers & Get Them to Experience Love & Fulfillment

10. <u>How to Pray for Your Children Everyday:</u> + 75 Powerful Prayers & Prophetic Declarations to Use and Pray for Your Children's Salvation, Future, Health, Education, Career, Relationship, Protection, etc

11. <u>How to Pray for Your Family:</u> + 70 Powerful Prayers and Prophetic Declarations for Your Family's Salvation, Healing, Victory, Breakthrough & Total Restoration.

12. <u>Daily Prayer Guide:</u> A Practical Guide to Praying and Getting Results – Learn How to Develop a Powerful Personal Prayer Life

13. <u>Make Him Respect You:</u> 31 Relationship Advice for Women to Make their Men Respect Them.

14. <u>How to Cast Out Demons from Your Home, Office and</u>

Property: 100 Powerful Prayers to Cleanse Your Home, Office, Land & Property from Demonic Attacks

15. Praying Through the Book of Psalms: Most Powerful Psalms and Powerful Prayers & Declarations for Every Situation: Birthday, Christmas, Business Ideas, Breakthrough, Deliverance, Healing, Comfort, Exams, Decision Making, Grief, and Many More.

16. STUDENTS' PRAYER BOOK: Powerful Motivation & Guide for Students & Anyone Preparing to Write Exams: Plus 10 Days of Powerful Prayers for Wisdom, Favor, Protection & Success in Studies, Exams & Life.

17. How to Pray and Receive Financial Miracle: Powerful Prayers for Financial Miracles, Business and Career Breakthrough

18. Prayers to Destroy Witchcraft Attacks Against Your Life & Family and Release Your Blessings

19. Deliverance from Marine Spirits: Powerful Prayers to Overcome Marine Spirits – Spirit Husbands and Spirit Wives – Permanently

20. Deliverance From Python Spirit: Powerful Prayers to Defeat

the Python Spirit – Spirit of Lies, Deceptions and Oppression.

21. <u>Anger Management God's Way</u>: Bible Ways to Control Your Emotions, Get Healed of Hurts & Respond to Offenses ...Plus Powerful Daily Prayers to Overcome Bad Anger Permanently

22. <u>How God Speaks to You</u>: An ABC Guide to Hearing the Voice of God & Following His Direction for Your Life

23. <u>Deliverance of the Mind</u>: Powerful Prayers to Deal With Mind Control, Fear, Anxiety, Depression, Anger and Other Negative Emotions | Gain Clarity & Peace of Mind & Manifest the Blessings of God

24. <u>26 Most Commonly Asked Questions About Demons:</u> All You Need to Know to Cast Out Demons, Obtain Deliverance for Yourself, For a Loved One or For Your Family

About the Author

Daniel Chika Okpara is a husband, father, pastor, businessman and lecturer. He has authored over 50 life transforming books on business, prayer, relationship and victorious living.

He is the president of Better Life World Outreach Centre - www.betterlifeworld.org - a non-denominational evangelism ministry committed to global prayer revival and evangelism.

Through the monthly Better Life Crusades, Better Life Health and Business Breakthrough Seminars and Better Life TV, thousands of lives have been won to the LORD, healed, blessed and restored to a purposeful living.

He holds a Master's Degree in Theology from Cornerstone Christian University and is married to Prophetess Doris, his prayer warrior, best friend and biggest support in life. They are blessed with two lovely kids

NOTES

26841177R00049

Printed in Great Britain
by Amazon